# T.I.P.S

## Techniques Ideas Principles & Strategies
### to turn difficult conversations into opportunity conversations

# Errol A Williams

# TIPS

## Techniques Ideas Principles & Strategies
*to turn difficult conversations into*
*opportunity conversations*

# Errol A Williams

For information please write to:
Scholar International
Bridge Park
Brentfield Harrow Road
Stonebridge Park
London NW10 0RG
Email: scholar.uk@virgin.net
Website: www.excelling.org

Book cover design by Errol A Williams

Published by Scholar International

ISBN 978-0-9532104-6-6

Dedicated to all the delegates that I
have had the honour and privilege to
share with and learn from since 1984.

# Delegates' Feedback

"*I* just wanted to let you know that I attended this training and Errol did not disappoint!! It has been THE most enlightening PCT training session that I have attended. Errol was a motivating presenter, using a coaching style and NLP principles to flexibly meet the needs of his audience. Very inspiring." Amanda

"Hi Errol. This was by far the best presented course I have attended and I have come back so eager to learn more and build upon what I have learned. In fact I switched off my favourite CD (Enrique Iglesias) and as my kids would tell you, that was really something and I revised everything I learned all the way home. I talked through everything I learned and it was so AMAZING how everything was jumping out at me: the notes all around the room, the pictures from the notes, phrases from the course, your fantastic stories. I really think I talked through everything, even the things that I could not recall when we were summarising during the three days. I was really amazed. On reaching home I couldn't stop talking about it!"

"The rapport that we struck up with you and the team as a whole was really great. Your teaching skills and personality, together with this rapport, really enabled us all to learn so much and thoroughly enjoy the three days. As I said I had only intended to stay till lunchtime on Friday as I had initially understood that it was a one day course and it was half-term week for my children but I was pleased to stay to the end, and we would all have stayed longer!!"

"I really look forward to a Refresher Course/Action Update, maybe in a year's time, as we discussed. As we said this would be most beneficial if held by you as our NLP tutor and would also be nice if the same group were to attend. I shall certainly be indicating to my employers that there will be a refresher course in preparation. Therefore once again THANK YOU for a fantastic course and the knowledge you imparted." Principal Auditor

"A real inspiration." Wales Audit Office

"One of the best (if not the best) trainer experiences I have had." London Borough of Enfield

"One of the best courses I have done." Waitrose

"Hi Errol. It's not often we take the time to say thank you to the people that have inspired us or have helped to shape our present/future. I would like to put that right and say a very big 'thank you' to you. When we first met (many, many, many years ago at South West Trains) you gave me a piece of advice that I have never forgotten; it's a piece of advice that I have embraced and have used it to make a significant impact on my life. The advice was, 'If you have a goal, write it down and put it on your fridge'. It sounds so simple and yet it has been so effective."

"Well, I did exactly as you said. I constantly set myself a series of personal goals and worked towards them. Since taking your advice I have achieved so much. I've ridden a camel across the Sinai Desert; I've watched the sun set over Mount Fuji; I've paid for someone else's groceries; jumped out of a plane; watched the sunrise over the Caribbean; bought a stranger a coffee; even took a helicopter into the Grand Canyon! There are many, many more things I could add to this list, but I think you get the point. By writing my goals down and looking at them every day, they became real."

"Thank you so much again. I have passed these words of wisdom on to so many people. I hope it helps them as much as it has helped me." Kevin

# CONTENTS

# Introduction

## Chapter One

$\mathcal{J}$ am delighted to have the opportunity to share my wealth of experience, on a topic that affects everyone.

I have worked with some of the largest companies to teach executives, senior managers, supervisors and others. What I am about to share are simple TIPS to turn difficult conversations into opportunity conversations.

**T**    Techniques
**I**    Ideas
**P**    Principles
**S**    Strategies

TIPS can be used in the work environment or personal life in general. When you go home and take out your keys, probably only one or at most two is needed to open the door. Maybe only one tip in this book is needed to vastly improve your life and ability to manage all difficult conversations.

Managing difficult conversations affects everyone in every generation, culture and age. It is impossible to go through life without having to manage difficult conversations.

**You may have to manage at least one
difficult conversation every week
for the rest of your life**

By applying the TIPS in this book, your return on investment will far outweigh the cost and time you spent. During the past ten years I have taught this course for companies for ninety minutes (Light Bites Learning) or a full day. During the course I always split the group and ask them to address these three points:

1.  List the most difficult conversations that you have ever had in this company
2.  List the reasons why you call them difficult conversations
3.  List the seven top TIPS for dealing with difficult conversations

Here are the top ten topics that managers find most difficult to address:

1.  Redundancy
2.  Personal hygiene
3.  Resistance to change
4.  Poor performance
5.  Performance reviews
6.  Disciplinary issues
7.  Mindset of upper managers
8.  Personality clashes or behaviour
9.  Negotiating
10. Managing peers

This list remains the same in every country, culture and company that I have been to. The good news is that we can develop the right attitude, skills and knowledge to address these difficult topics.

Managers gave a variety of reasons why they found these topics difficult to deal with. Here are the top two:

1.  They perceived that the other person may respond negatively
2.  Managers confessed that they did not have the right Attitude, Skills and Knowledge (ASK) to deal with these difficulties

Here are the top ten TIPS that managers give for dealing with difficult conversations. This list has remained the same for over ten years:

1.  Listen actively
2.  Remain calm and maintain self control
3.  Stay focused and do not be manipulated
4.  Be assertive, respectful and professional

5.   Be prepared and always have all the facts

6.   Choose an appropriate time and place

7.   Be prepared for bad reactions

8.   Be honest and confidential

9.   Prepare people for bad news

10.  Document and follow up

# Listen Actively

## Chapter Two

*L*istening actively is one of the most powerful TIPS you will ever need to manage difficult conversations. Use these six TIPS when listening:

| | |
|---|---|
| **L** | Look interested |
| **I** | Inquire with questions |
| **S** | Stay on target |
| **T** | Test your understanding |
| **E** | Evaluate the whole message |
| **N** | Neutralise or control your feelings |

## Look Interested

During a difficult conversation, show the other person that they are the most important person in the world. Treat them as you would the Queen or King of your country. Sit up, turn off the phone, stop using the computer and make an effort to treat them as royalty. Maintain eye contact, nod your head, give acknowledging responses and smile where necessary.

Supposing you were chosen to accompany the royal family, to represent your country or company before the world press. During the Queen's response to you, your phone rang and you answered it. What do you think the press would report about you, your company or country?

## Inquire With Questions

The quality of your learning is determined by the quality of the questions that you ask. You cannot make wise decisions with poor information. General Colin Powell, the former Secretary of State in the United States said,

"Don't take action if you have only enough information to give you less than a 40% chance of being right, but don't wait until you have enough facts to be 100% sure, because by then it is almost always too late. Today, excessive delay in the name of information-gathering breeds 'analysis paralysis'. Procrastination in the name of reducing risk actually increases risk."

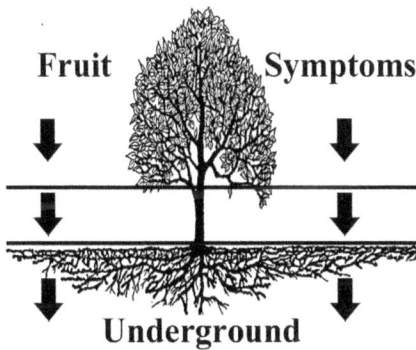

The most important part of a tree is not the fruit it produces but the underground element, the root. If you cut down the part of the tree that produces the fruit or the trunk, it could still grow back. However, if you destroy the root you destroy the tree completely. The arrows in the above diagram represent your questions. Ask as many questions as you feel are necessary. Never give advice or make a decision until you believe you have got to the "root of the matter." To give an answer before you fully understand the whole matter is foolish and could cause much harm. The art of asking questions is a skill that is worth developing. Ask open, closed, probing, fact-based and leading questions. Operate like a judge. Never send out the jury until both prosecution and defence have finished their questioning. In most cases you are the prosecution, defence, jury and judge.

**Stay On Target**

During a difficult conversation never allow yourself to be manipulated or sidetracked, stay focused. If you have three agenda items to discuss and the other person introduces two more, note them. Then get back to your agenda and deal with each item one at a time. Be assertive, confident, firm, empathic and friendly. It is tempting to go from one agenda item to another, wasting time and taking longer to make decisions. Time is money, invest it wisely.

## Test Your Understanding

Imagine spending weeks on a task, only to discover you completed the wrong task, because you did not test your understanding. Never make the assumption that you understand what is said to you. Assumption is the mother of most conflicts. Conflict often increases in the workplace or home because of misunderstanding.

Test your understanding and the other person's in order to guarantee that you are both on the same page. Failure to do so could lead to misunderstanding, confusion and conflict. Repeat what you have heard in your own language, verbally or by email. Never be afraid or intimidated to test, test, test. Turn to Chapter 9, Master Feedback for more on this subject.

## Evaluate The Whole Message

During a difficult conversation there are only three channels through which the whole message is communicated. They are:

1.  Body language     55%
2.  Tone of voice     38%
3.  Words             7%

The above research of Albert Mehrabian shows the order of priority and the percentage of information gathered from each channel. Most people when communicating focus more on what is said, the 7%, rather than how it is said, the 93%.

However, 93% of the information gathered is sent sub-consciously. Most of the time we are unaware what our body or tone of voice is saying to the other person. When you are on the phone the percentage changes to, tone of voice 86% and words 14%. Always remember that your body is always speaking.

People's thoughts and feelings are often conveyed through their body language and tone of voice. Therefore, always observe and evaluate the whole message that is sent by you and the other person. When considering body language here are the six areas to watch out for:

- Mouth
- Appearance
- Gestures
- Posture
- Voice
- Eye movement

When you speak, how is your facial expression? Are you smiling, is your jaw too tight or relaxed? Always check your appearance in a mirror and ask yourself, "what impression do I give dressed this way?"

Does the movement of your body, especially your hands, support what you say? Is your posture straight, upright or are you slouched, too near, too far, slumped or positioned higher or lower than the other person? Do you mumble, complain, criticise, beat around the bush, or do you get straight to the point, clearly, directly and specifically? Is your tone acceptable with the right Rhythm, Speed, Volume and Pitch (RSVP)? Do you vary the rhythm to make it interesting? Do you speak at the right pace (e.g., 100 words per minute) to arrest your listener's attention? Do you project your voice and vary your pitch in order to be understood? Do you look confidently into other people's eyes, or do you gaze at the ceiling, floor or other objects? Be wise, support what you say by how you say it. Finally, stay far from words that stir up strife, anger and confusion. Speak warm, friendly and easy words that your audience understands.

## Neutralise Or Control Your Feelings

For some it is easier to fly an aircraft, go to the moon, build a mobile phone, automobile or a mansion than it is to control their feelings. This is one of the hardest things for human beings to do.

If you want people to talk to you, listen more, talk less and control your anger. Becoming angry will discourage people from communicating with you. Those who have no control over their anger make it difficult for others to talk to them. You must always be in control of your thoughts, words and actions.

Listen to others when they wish to express their feelings. Often the feelings of the speaker are more important than the spoken word.

Imagine that you have three very important things to tell your manager. The second and third things are the worst, so you decide to start with the easiest one. During the conversation about the first item, your manager immediately becomes angry and abusive. He starts to shout and accuse you and throws his chair across the desk. Would you at that time raise the second and third items?

Do you know someone that you have never been able to share items two and three with? You may be working with colleagues or living with people who have never shared items two and three with you. Are you preventing people from talking to you? Are you bringing pain or pleasure to your conversations? Whoever or whatever brings pain or discomfort, we tend to avoid. On the other hand we gravitate towards pleasure like bees to honey.

Many years ago I told my darling wife that she could never upset me again. I did not say that I would never become angry or upset again. What I meant was this: if I do become angry I would take total responsibility for my feelings and actions. I would tell myself that I made myself angry and upset. Are you blaming others for your thoughts, feelings, words and actions because of how they are behaving? It is not what happens to you in life that matters most, it is how you respond to what happens. Do not reduce yourself to other people's dysfunction.

Picture yourself being excited and overwhelmed with joy after your manager gives you an excellent report of yourself. A few weeks later he reprimands you unfairly and you break down in tears and end up having to take tablets for depression. If this continues time after time, who is in control of you?

Never give control of who you are to any other person. If you do you may pay a great price. Here is a simple tip to help calm yourself down. Create a playlist of your five favourite songs, then play them to yourself when you are feeling low. Music is one of the most powerful ways to calm down an angry person. Listening to music can reduce chronic pain by up to 21% and depression by up to 25%, according to an article in the UK based *Journal of Advanced Nursing.*

**Barriers To Listening**

Most barriers to effective listening can be placed under the following headings:

- Assumptions
- Roaming mind
- External and internal distractions
- Your interpretation and distortion
- Oversensitivity
- Unclear speaker
- Unforgiving

## Assumptions

Impatient listeners spend a great deal of time interrupting and finishing off other people's sentences. Presumptuous listeners feel that they know better and that the views of others are an interruption of their own. They think only of themselves and are good at faking attention. They are always preoccupied with what to say next when they are listening to others. They miss the true feelings that are being experienced and the nonverbal signals which can reveal more than the spoken word. Before you begin a difficult conversation never assume the worst.

## Roaming Mind

The brain has the ability to wander off aimlessly while listening to others. A roaming and uncontrolled mind will find it hard to concentrate and stay on target. If a subject is boring, poor listeners will allow their minds to drift, then return their attention to the speaker. While a person is talking, a roaming mind will dwell on the past, present problems or future dreams. This pattern could continue throughout a person's entire life if they fail to master the art of listening.

## External And Internal Distractions

Interruptions, noise, movement, the telephone, discomfort and an unpleasant atmosphere are some of the external distractions one can experience. Unhealthiness, sickness, hearing difficulties, tiredness and pain are some of the internal distractions that stop us from listening effectively. Unless these distractions are minimised or controlled, listening will always be affected.

## Your Interpretation And Distortion

One of the greatest barriers to effective listening is interpretation and distortion. Because words mean different things to different people, it is easy to misunderstand a sentence, let alone a whole message. Many conflicts in the workplace could be avoided if people listened actively to each other. Poor listeners often fail to ask the right questions to aid their understanding.

Their preconceived ideas about the speaker's beliefs, views, opinions, lifestyle, personality and background affect how they listen and distort the message. In many situations our past experiences have affected the way we listen to others. How are you interpreting what is said to you? Are you 100% certain that you fully understand what is said to you?

## Oversensitivity

Many people become oversensitive because of what they hear, see or experience. They are easily able to close their minds, completely switch off and ultimately stop listening. They become angry, frustrated, are quick tempered and get annoyed very easily. They do not know how to neutralise or control their feelings. In this state of confusion, the speaker and listener will find it very difficult to continue communicating effectively. When you become oversensitive and angry you are making a difficult conversation more difficult.

## Unclear Speaker

Unclear speakers make it very difficult and painful for their listeners to listen. Often they speak too slowly or too fast. Some speakers use words that are hard to understand and long sentences. Their accent, style, poor presentation and mannerisms help to block effective listening, wasting time, energy and money. Those who have speech impediments, or for whom English is a second language, will have to work harder at being understood.

## Unforgiving

Unforgiving is like drinking poison and hoping that the other person will die from it. To forgive is to set a prisoner free and actually discover the prisoner was YOU! If you fail to forgive others you are doing greater harm to yourself. Unforgiving can increase your stress levels and can lead to all kinds of sicknesses. Are you destroying your career, health and relationships with the poison of unforgiving?

It is emotionally draining to manage a difficult conversation with someone you will not forgive or who will not forgive you. If you have been offended by your manager, colleagues, customers or others it is vitally important that you decide to forgive. To forgive is to pardon, cease to hold anger or resentment against someone. If you have hurt someone, it is important to apologise and to mean it.

The big question is, how does a person forgive another? Forgiving someone is not a feeling, it is simply a decision that you make. You must decide:

• I will pardon
• I will not hold anger or resentment

Only you can make the decision to forgive and you have the ability to do so.

**The Secret Of Listening**

My organisation was once badly affected by the mistake of another organisation. I was outraged as the receptionist answered the telephone. After introducing myself I said to the receptionist, "Your company is totally incompetent", to which she replied, "I am sorry Mr Williams, we do take responsibility and will correct the situation immediately."

I responded angrily with, "I am sorry? Sorry is not good enough, I should never have done business with your company." Again she replied, "I am sorry Mr Williams, I do understand, we do take responsibility and will correct the situation immediately." Now I was fuming as I said angrily, "How do you mean you understand? You do not understand, if you understood I would not be in this mess."

She did not interrupt as she listened and calmly responded again with, "Mr Williams we do take responsibility and will correct the situation immediately." Suddenly

I realised how foolish I was behaving. Her self control, assertiveness, consistency and positive approach led me to realise how unprofessionally I was behaving.

Steve, a delegate on one of our Managing Difficult Conversation courses said, "Be so positive that you make it difficult for other people to be difficult to you." Are you making it easy for people to be difficult to you?

Let me share one more story.

As I was chairing a management meeting, a female voluntary worker stormed into the room and began to swear and shout. Her behaviour shocked everyone in the room. At the end of the meeting I sent for her and asked her to justify her actions. Within a matter of minutes we were able to resolve the situation. I listened with empathy, sought information by asking questions, summarised then paraphrased her response in my own words. I also targeted my conversation, evaluated the whole message, neutralised and controlled my feelings. My interpersonal skills, nonverbal communication and genuineness totally overwhelmed her. Several weeks later she was a delegate on one of our training programmes. At the end of running the listening skills session, I decided to do a role play. The purpose of the role play was to demonstrate how to listen more effectively. I called for a volunteer to do a role play with me but no one came forward. After a little while most delegates suggested that the same girl should volunteer. They felt that she would give me a greater challenge. She refused.

I will never forget her response. "I am not doing anything with Errol Williams because he makes me look stupid." "The other day", she continued, "I walked into his office, shouting and behaving badly and he just sat there and listened to me."

When you use this powerful listening skill you will:

1.  Cause others to take a good look at themselves
2.  Make friends very easily
3.  Save time, money and embarrassment
4.  Feel self-controlled, powerful and in charge

5.  Increase in knowledge, understanding and wisdom
6.  Be more compassionate towards others
7.  Grow in confidence
8.  Find that people will respect and admire you, because you know how to listen to them
9.  Love listening to others
10. Find it easy to socialise with others
11. Feel good about yourself

**One of the greatest TIPS in listening:**
**listen more, speak less and**
**control your anger**

*(The memory aid LISTEN is taken from Melrose Film Productions Limited)*

# Use The 10/80/10 Structure

## Chapter Three

*H*aving a structure to manage difficult conversations makes a huge difference. If you do not follow a specific structure as you make your delivery, the other party will have a difficult time keeping up with you. One of the most simple and effective structures for any type of presentation is, the beginning, middle and end.

### Beginning

Use the following memory aid, INTRO to set the scene at the beginning of all difficult conversations:

**I**    Interest

**N**    Need

**T**    Timing

**R**    Response

**O**    Objective

At the beginning of your conversation arouse the interest of the other person and find out what needs they have. Always remember that the other person's favourite radio station is WII.FM (What's In It For Me?) Let them know how long the meeting or conversation will last and give them an idea as to when they can respond with questions or comments. Finally, agree the objectives. The INTRO allows you to set the scene perfectly.

**Middle**

The middle is the main part of your conversation or presentation. It should follow a logical path that is easy for the other party to follow. The 4 P's is an easy technique to remember and use. This tip can be used with any kind of presentation that you do.

**P**    Position

**P**    Problem

**P**    Possibilities

**P**    Proposal

Highlight the overall position. Explain the problem and its current and future effects. Show the many possibilities and finally, make your specific proposal. *(The 4 P's from Video Arts)*

## End

The ending is as important as the beginning or the middle, therefore plan to CLOSE effectively.

**C**    Conclusion

**L**    Link

**O**    Objective

**S**    Summary

**E**    Emotion (questions and answers)

Saying at the end of the meeting or conversation, "in conclusion", lets everyone know that you are ending the discussion. Link any key points, review the objectives, summarise the decisions and give an opportunity for questions and answers. Some pilots say that the hardest part of flying any aircraft is the take-off and landing. You can vastly improve your ability to handle difficult conversations by mastering the beginning, middle and end.

The 10/80/10 technique is very simple. Spend 10% of the overall time of the meeting on the beginning or INTRO. Spend 80% of the time on the middle or 4 P's. Finally, spend 10% on the ending or CLOSE. For a thirty minute meeting the INTRO and CLOSE should take approximately three minutes each.

**Following this simple technique will give you control, boost your confidence and help to maintain order**

# Manage Difficult Conversations Quickly

## Chapter Four

*P*rocrastination means to deliberately delay or put something off until another time. Unwise procrastination is a thief of time.

Imagine that you are preparing a celebration meal for your entire extended family. You look around to check on little Jimmy, your eighteen-month-old son, who is playing with matches beside the curtains. Time is against you and you cannot stop what you are doing, so you leave him to play. Ten minutes later you look around to notice that little Jimmy has lit several matches. You notice the potential danger but you decide not to stop because the family will be arriving shortly. To your amazement, fifteen minutes later your kitchen is on fire. Now you only have time to grab little Jimmy and run for safety. When the fire brigade arrive, your house and half the street are on fire. Therefore the fire officer had to call four other neighbouring stations to assist.

This fire could have been prevented if you had taken the matches from little Jimmy the first time you saw them. Now think of the damage, cost and inconvenience because of your unwise procrastination. Do not deliberately delay or ignore difficult conversations that must be dealt with. Manage them quickly before they escalate out of control. Managers who postpone difficult conversations may end up having to involve:

- Other employees
- Directors
- Tribunal panel
- The press
- Customers
- Family members

Dealing too quickly with difficult conversations when you are unprepared, can cause even greater damage. Therefore, prepare yourself well and have all the necessary facts. Always remember to obey this tip: "Preparation, preparation, preparation". The 7 P's below are often used in project planning or when training for life or death situations.

- Prior
- Proper
- Preparation
- Prevents
- Painfully
- Poor
- Performance

It is cheaper to build a fence at the top of the cliff than to pay for an ambulance at the bottom.

Here is a powerful technique to use with difficult conversations:

**F**    File it
**A**    Action it
**T**    Trash it

## File It

There will be times when you will have more than one difficult conversation to manage. Managing them all simultaneously is impractical. Make a decision which ones to delay and set a time in your diary when to deal with them. In other words file it. Use procrastination wisely.

## Action It

Difficult conversations that are urgent, important or critical must be actioned quickly. In some cases delegate it. Never delegate to dump but rather delegate to develop. As a manager, you are only delegating the responsibility and not the accountability. If anything goes wrong you will be held accountable. Therefore, action it yourself or delegate wisely and give all the necessary support.

**Trash It**

Generals do not go to war if there is no spoil to gain. Avoid fruitless and unnecessary difficult conversations like the plague. They waste time, money, effort, energy and achieve nothing. Time is money, invest it wisely.

Judge wisely which difficult conversations you will delay, action, delegate or even avoid completely. Use FAT for all difficult conversations, paper management and emails also in order to:

**S**   Save
**Y**   Your
**S**   Self
**T**   Time
**E**   Energy
**M**   Money

# Be Calm
# And
# Assertive

## Chapter Five

*A*ssertive people state their needs, wants, feelings, opinions or beliefs in a clear, direct, specific, honest and loving way and not at the expense of others.

- Assertive people are honest with themselves and with others
- They are confident and positive
- They aim to first understand other people, rather than trying to get others to understand them
- They behave in a rational adult way
- They negotiate and reach workable compromises in most difficult situations

- They are in control of how they think, feel, speak and act
- They are always able to say "yes" or "no" without feeling ashamed or guilty and without having to justify their answers

Here are seven TIPS for being calm and assertive under extreme pressure. They will improve lives and build better working relationships.

**Decide What To Say, Then Be Clear, Direct And Specific**

- Give yourself enough time to think carefully
- Speak firmly, calmly, using a reasonable tone and a steady pace
- Do not be vague, abrupt or rude; be direct and clear
- Do not beat around the bush, get straight to the point

## Examine The Response

- Listen actively with empathy to others
- Indicate that you have heard and understood
- Do not become aggressive or passive
- Remain calm

## Compromise

- Settle differences by mutual agreement
- Develop and use your negotiating skills
- Be reasonable and flexible

## Interpersonal Skills Must Be Used

- Communicate accurately, clearly and effectively
- Be confident, positive and present yourself genuinely and professionally
- Stay away from resentment, confusion and anger
- Control and direct your body language and tone of voice positively

## Do Not Be Manipulated Or Side-Tracked

- Be repetitive and persistent
- Be aware of what is happening and stay on target without being stubborn
- Do not allow others to make you feel undermined, guilty or patronised

## Eliminate Negative Situations Positively

- Deal with hostility and all criticisms positively
- Always control your thoughts, feelings, words and actions
- Treat every situation in life as a major opportunity
- Never attack or verbally abuse the other person

## Disclose Your Feelings

- Do not be afraid to state how you feel
- Do not use argumentative language, i.e. "You make me angry." "You are to blame." "You, you, you"

- Use "I" statements, "I feel angry", "I am annoyed"
- Think carefully before you speak

Use this memory aid to remember the seven TIPS.

**D**    Decide What To Say, Then Be Clear, Direct And Specific

**E**    Examine The Response

**C**    Compromise

**I**    Interpersonal Skills Must Be Used

**D**    Do Not Be Manipulated Or Side-Tracked

**E**    Eliminate Negative Situations Positively

**D**    Disclose Your Feelings

## The Four Life Positions

*(Eric Berne)*

Passive, aggressive, paralysis and assertive are the four life positions from which we communicate to others.

**Passive People**

- Believe that others are better than themselves
- Do not get straight to the point
- Are shy, easy to "give up" and surrender
- Spend time feeling inadequate and being depressed
- Are the perfect target for an aggressive person
- Often find themselves saying, "I am sorry, please help me"
- Use the common phrase: "You're ok, I'm not ok"

One of the most difficult things for a passive person to do is to get straight to the point. They spend much time beating around the bush and living within themselves. They also find it difficult to say how they feel, thereby adding to feelings already stored up inside. They often find it extremely difficult to socialise with other people and are the perfect target for the aggressive person.

A passive person may reject positive feedback by saying, "I could have done better." "I do not deserve it."

## Aggressive People

- Believe that they are better than others
- Are autocratic and bossy
- Find it hard to listen and trust others
- Spend time telling off others and finding faults
- Are often very frustrated and unhappy
- Have only a few friends
- Do not know how to cope with an assertive person
- Use the common phrase: "I'm ok, you're not ok"

Beware of aggressive people who present themselves disguised as an assertive person. They appear to be assertive but inwardly they are ravening wolves dressed in sheep's clothing. They will deceive you.

How will you know such an aggressive person? It is very simple. Let me explain. You will know them by the way they act, just as you can identify a tree by its fruit. Different kinds of trees can quickly be identified by examining their fruit.

You are not assertive because you look assertive, but your motive and action must be brought into question. If you are hurtful, manipulative, make people feel guilty, lie or use conniving means, then you are not assertive, you are aggressive.

**Paralysis People**

- Do not believe in themselves or in others
- Often feel suicidal
- Spend time complaining, withdrawn, depressed and feel a sense of total hopelessness
- Do nothing constructive with their time and life
- Believe the world will end soon, "so why bother"
- Use the common phrase: "I'm not ok, you're not ok"

Paralysis is the worst life position to be in. It is the inability to function properly because of psychological injury or sickness. Psychological injury can occur due to the death of a loved one or any other similar situation.

This person has given up on life, the community and others. They feel that no one cares for them, even though they are told, "I love you." They are easily affected by their circumstances because of the negative way they view their lives.

## Assertive People

- Are friendly, honest and peaceable
- Find it easy to get on with others
- Spend time enjoying life, work, friends and family
- Are often happy, pleasant and fun to be with
- Are very understanding
- Use the common phrase: "I'm ok, you're ok"

Be assertive, calm, professional and relaxed during difficult conversations. Be aware of your own emotions and manage yourself professionally.

No one can manage or control you but you. Therefore:

| | | |
|---|---|---|
| **B**uild | on your | **S**trengths |
| **E**liminate | your | **W**eaknesses |
| **E**xploit | your | **O**pportunities |
| **R**emove | all | **T**hreats |

Build on your strengths and eliminate weaknesses with identified training needs. Take advantage of opportunities when they come and remove or minimise all threats.

Of the four life positions, where do you spend most of your time? Or, in other words, where do you live? One delegate put it this way, "I live at Aggressive Street but from time to time I go to visit Passive and Assertive Streets." Another delegate said, "I spend most of my time and life being passive but on occasions I get aggressive and feel in a state of paralysis." "90% of the time when I communicate with others I am aggressive", said another delegate. What about you? To be passive, aggressive or experience paralysis, will waste your time, your life and that of others.

# Negotiate Effectively

## Chapter Six

*A*ll negotiation is communication. The better you are at communicating, the better you will become at negotiating. Negotiation tip number one, where appropriate get it in writing. Excellent negotiation skills help to gather support, win the confidence of others and improve chances for success.

Being prepared and physically at ease makes the negotiation process flow more smoothly and effectively. Use these TIPS that top executives use during difficult conversations.

## Nonverbal Communication

- Be conscious of the messages that your body sends out
- Be sure to observe closely the messages being sent via the other person's body language
- Be wise, support what you say by how you say it

## Effective Listening And Communication

- Listen actively with empathy and build rapport before the negotiation begins
- Ask questions and listen closely to words used and feelings expressed
- Be sure to communicate Accurately, Clearly and Effectively (ACE)

## Goals And Values

- Establish your goals and put them in order of importance
- Find out what the other party really wants

- Do not go against your values or expect others to go against theirs

## Our Solution

- Create and stick to an agenda and where appropriate get decisions in writing
- Be fair, flexible and prepared to give up some ground
- Remember, the key is not my solution or your solution but our solution, aim for a win-win

## Tactics

- Beware of tactics that are used to manipulate, side-track or influence you
- Do not rush and make rash decisions. If a deadlock looks hopeless, buy time
- Never use a tactic if it will affect a relationship

There are many good and bad tactics to negotiation. It is your responsibility to be fully aware of them and know how to counteract them. Here are some tactics that are used frequently.

## The Ladder Approach

Discuss and resolve easier issues first, then work your way up to the more difficult issues last.

## Silence Is Golden

Keeping silent is an art that many people find extremely difficult to do. Yet, it is one of the most powerful strategies in active listening.

Do not use your silence to plan what you are going to say next. Use it to understand what others are saying. Learn from the old saying: "You learn more with your mouth closed and your ears open."

"Never forget the power of silence, that massively disconcerting pause which goes on and on and may at last induce an opponent to babble and backtrack nervously." *(Lance Morrow)*

## Walk Out

During the negotiation you may choose a strategic point to leave or close the meeting.

## Limited Authority

During the negotiation you declare that you do not have the authority to make the final decision. The way to counter limited authority is to seek to negotiate from the beginning, with the person who has the final say.

## Feel, Felt, Found

I understand the way you feel, I have felt the same way before but I found that this is the best way forward.

## The Delay

When it is time to make a decision, tell the other person that you will think it over and get back to him/her. While you are thinking it over, get advice from others and sleep on it. When it is time to decide you will be in a better position to do so.

## Integrity

- Always honour your word, let your yes be yes and your no be no
- Be honest and faithful
- Treat others the way you want them to treat you

## Assertiveness

- State your needs, wants, feelings, opinions or beliefs in a clear, direct, specific, honest and loving way
- Do not be passive, aggressive or appear in a state of paralysis, be confident
- Be positive at all times

## Think And Reflect

- Always think ahead before agreeing to anything
- Continuously review what is going on before, during and after the negotiation
- Be creative and imaginative, if there is a stalemate find the underlying cause

## Interpersonal Development

- The largest room in the world is the room for improvement. Build on your strengths and eliminate your weaknesses with the right training
- Continually develop your Attitude, Skills and Knowledge (ASK)
- Read books, study training materials, watch videos, surf the internet, attend seminars and listen to experts

## Neutralise Or Control Your Feelings

- Control the way you think, feel, talk, act and do not take things personally
- Always remain calm, self-controlled, honest and professional
- Listen more, speak less and control your anger

## Game Plan

- Do your research, prepare in advance and determine your bottom line goal
- Be creative and come up with more than one alternative
- Use the rule of three: Maximum, Ideal and Minimum (MIM)

You should know what course of action will be taken if the negotiations fail and an agreement cannot be reached. Before you enter a negotiation, you should always have at least three figures or positions worked out, Maximum, Ideal and Minimum.

1.  The maximum is the most that you could possibly achieve from the negotiation
2.  The ideal is the figure that you are really after, anything between 60 to 80% of the maximum
3.  The minimum is your bottom line, the lowest possible figure or position that you would settle for

"You must never try to make all the money that's in a deal. Let the other fellow make some money too, because if you have a reputation for always making all the money, you won't have many deals." *(J. Paul Getty, American oil tycoon)*

## Negotiating

**N**    Nonverbal Communication

**E**    Effective Listening And Communication

**G**    Goals And Values

**O**    Our Solution

**T**    Tactics

**I**    Integrity

**A**    Assertiveness

**T**    Think And Reflect

**I**    Interpersonal Development

**N**    Neutralise Or Control Your Feelings

**G**    Game Plan

# Approach
# Management
# Wisely

## Chapter Seven

*H*aving a difficult conversation with your boss does not have to be a frightening experience. Turn the fear around to your advantage. Firstly, change your mindset and view it as a positive opportunity conversation. Picture this as a wonderful opportunity to show your ability and an excellent training and learning experience.

Secondly, use the many TIPS in this book to assist you. The more you use them, the more confident you will become and the easier it gets. Even the people around you will learn to manage difficult conversations better, when they see your excellent examples. Here are some of the most difficult conversation topics that staff have with their bosses:

1.  Challenging the boss's attitude and behaviour
2.  Challenging the boss's decisions
3.  Requesting a pay rise
4.  Seeking a promotion
5.  Asking for feedback
6.  Agreeing targets

Finally, here is another tip that could greatly boost your confidence and give you the results you are after. Take your boss to the BAR.

**B**   Benefits
**A**   Advantages
**R**   Results

Before you approach your boss do your preparation, preparation, preparation. To simply pick up the phone or rush into a meeting without any preparation is called an ambush.

**Step 1**

Choose your subject and make a complete list of all the benefits, advantages and results if things were to change. This list will become your agenda. Always remember, whoever sets the agenda controls the meeting.

**Step 2**

Put the list in order of priority and put the top two benefits first. You are now applying the 80/20 principle that states, 80% of the benefits come from 20% of the causes. The other 20% of benefits come from the 80% of causes. This principle is used by companies around the world and can be applied to your work and personal life.

In business the principle states, 80% of sales come from 20% of the customers. The other 20% of sales come from 80% of the customers. Therefore spend 80% of your time, effort and resources on the 20% of customers that give you the greater benefits. *(The Pareto principle)*

**Step 3**

Request a meeting and choose the time, place and environment that will positively contribute to your cause. The timing is critical, so choose wisely. Do not choose a time when you suspect the boss is unhappy or under pressure. If possible meet in a neutral place and not in your boss's office.

Do not be late for the meeting. If your meeting is to start at 2pm and you arrive at 2pm you are late. If you arrive at 1:30pm you are on time. If you arrive after 2pm it is unacceptable. If you ask for fifteen minutes, only take fourteen.

**Step 4**

Consider every possible question or objection that your boss may have and prepare answers for them. If possible rehearse the meeting with a trusted colleague or family member. Two or three smart brains are always better than one.

## Step 5

Speak from the heart with empathy, passion, brevity, clarity and effectiveness. Use the KISS principle that states, Keep It Short and Simple. Listen actively and talk less. After your introduction, begin with points one and two and summarise and close with points one and two. What is emphasised most and said last will be remembered most. Accept the outcome with grace and dignity because you are not the boss or the decision maker.

## Step 6

Despite the outcome of the meeting, thank your boss for his/her time and consideration. This demonstrates that you have approached the situation with professionalism, respect and class. After all, you may have to hold this meeting or a similar one on another day with your boss.

# Step 7

Ensure the outcome of your meeting is put in writing and do not forget to follow up where necessary.

# Manage Acute Stress Effectively

## Chapter Eight

*F*ailing to manage difficult conversations effectively could lead to acute stress in you and others. Acute stress is pressure, strain or tension that tends to deform the body. It can cause a mentally, physically or emotionally disruptive or disquieting influence. To its victims it is severe, painful, distressing, confusing, depressing and hard to endure. Its final goal is to destroy your career, your life and those around you.

How you react to problems, challenges or situations that you face, will determine how much stress you experience. It is commonly reported by experts on stress, that not all stress is bad or fatal. Just like eating is not bad, but eating too much can be fatal. Stress is a part of life and an everyday experience that can be of benefit to us. Playing a game of tennis with your colleague produces a little stress, which is normal. When we feel sad, angry, jealous or embarrassed we experience stress. However, there is a big difference between normal everyday stress and acute stress.

Acute stress has caused much damage to people because difficult conversations were not managed effectively. If you experience acute stress, you could suffer from major physical sickness, emotional disorders and even experience burn out.

Some of the most commonly reported physical sicknesses are high blood pressure, strokes, kidney failure and heart attacks. Doctors warn us that continuous pressure in any of these four areas will lead to other sicknesses, diseases and eventually death. Acute stress also affects our behaviour. It causes some to increase smoking, drinking, shouting and being angry. It has also destroyed many relationships and caused people to become worried, depressed, frustrated, lonely, aggressive, hostile and suicidal. Why get angry, frustrated and depressed over something that you cannot change? If you can change it, change it. Being honest with yourself is the first step to recovering from acute stress. Here are some acute stress avoidance or relieving TIPS:

1. Get adequate sleep
2. Exercise regularly
3. Plan your day and only do what you can manage
4. Take short breaks throughout the day
5. Travel well ahead of time
6. Think before you take action
7. Get professional help and share your problems with someone you can trust
8. Be assertive
9. Build relaxation time into your day
10. Do breathing exercises at least three times a day
11. Have a proper balanced diet and do not forget the fruit and vegetables

12. Cut down or stop drinking alcohol and stop taking unnecessary drugs
13. Go on holiday
14. Be quick to listen
15. Socialise with others and have fun
16. Set goals for your life
17. Make your week interesting
18. Stop foolish thoughts from entering your mind or do not entertain thoughts which are unproductive

One of the most important things about minimising, controlling and eliminating acute stress, is to control your thinking. When you control your thoughts, you automatically control the way you feel and act and the results you achieve. When you control your thoughts, you feel at ease, comfortable and peaceful. The complete opposite to how you would feel, if you suffered from acute stress.

Here are two important TIPS to bear in mind when delivering bad news to others,

1.   Always prepare people to receive bad news
2.   Be prepared for bad reactions

Prepare yourself and do not spring the information on them suddenly. You may start off by saying: "Paul, I am sorry to be the bearer of bad news", or "Paul, what I am about to share with you is not pleasant." Although you have indicated that the news is not pleasant, you have not yet revealed what it is. In so doing, you have given the person time to prepare themselves. Once you believe that they are prepared, get straight to the point.

Your inability to manage difficult conversations effectively, may result in you hurting and destroying yourself and others.

Here is another warning and a helpful tip

**A**    Acute Stress

**C**    Causes

**U**    Untold

**T**    Threats

**E**    Every Time


**S**    So

**T**    Think

**R**    Responsibly

**E**    Every

**S**    Single

**S**    Second

# Master Feedback

## Chapter Nine

*I*t is vitally important that you master the giving and receiving of feedback. We work in a multicultural environment where different words, body language and tone of voice mean different things to different people. If we do not master feedback there will be misunderstanding, confusion, conflict and loss of opportunities.

A train driver was disciplined for not giving feedback to instructions that he received. His failure to give proper feedback led to a train derailment. Are your conversations being derailed because of poor feedback?

Train companies have many safety warnings in place such as: Drivers Reminder Appliance or Train Protection and Warning System. These systems and many more are in place for staff and passenger safety. Here is a safety warning for dealing with difficult conversations, master feedback or you may pay a great price.

During the second World War a misunderstanding occurred over just one phrase, *"table it"*. It caused great debate and ill will. Sir Winston Churchill writes about the confusion between the American and British military leaders during the Second World War. In his book, The Second World War, Volume 3, *The Grand Alliance*, he wrote:

"There were however differences of expression in the early days which led to an amusing incident. The British Staff prepared a paper which they wished to raise as a matter of urgency, and informed their American colleagues that they wished to 'table it'. To the American Staff 'tabling' a paper meant putting it away in a drawer and forgetting it. A long and even acrimonious argument ensued before both parties realized that they were agreed on the merits and wanted the same thing."

To demonstrate the power of feedback, during my Managing Difficult Conversation courses, I always say to the delegates, "Without asking for any feedback, please follow the instructions that I am about to give three times. Draw a small eye and dot it." These were the responses that I received from fourteen managers on the same course:

1. i
2.
3. i it
4. .
5. ii
6. it
7. it
8. iii
9. it.
10. i it

This is what I meant: ït

There was confusion over whether I was referring to i or an eye. Of the fourteen managers in the room there were ten different interpretations. Notice also that everyone interprets a part of the message correctly but not the whole message. Every time you communicate, especially during difficult conversations, misunderstanding could occur. During difficult conversations decide when to give feedback and when to ask for it. You may say the following:

- What do you understand so far?
- Could you please repeat that for me?
- What do you mean by the use of that word?
- Let me summarise what I understand
- If I understand you correctly what you are saying is ...

Communication is a three-way process of sending, receiving and giving feedback. If there is no feedback then there is no guarantee that the receiver has fully understood the sender. Good feedback guarantees understanding between both parties. It also enhances achievements and fosters better working relationships. The education institution and the business world are in tune with the value of effective feedback. Between them they have invested millions to get it right. The feedback stages in the:

• Education institution is exams or tests
• Business world is evaluation or review

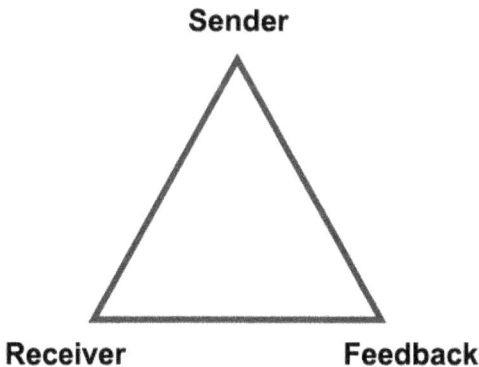

Both sender and receiver are responsible for giving or asking for feedback.

# Develop
# Your
# ASK

## Chapter Ten

$\mathcal{M}$any conflicts in the workplace escalate because they are not managed properly. By developing the right Attitude, Skills and Knowledge (ASK) you:

- Increase your worth and value in the market place
- Become more confident and feel empowered
- Resolve conflicts more quickly and easily
- Will save your company thousands of pounds
- Will increase productivity, reduce stress and a host of other negative influences
- Will gain greater customer satisfaction and retention

Every occupation on the planet, from the cleaner to the Prime Minister are based around these three areas.

Attitude
Skills
Knowledge

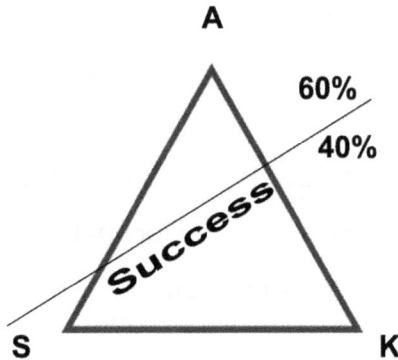

Every question at your interview probably came under one of these three headings, Attitude, Skills and Knowledge. Interviews are generally to find out the following: Who you are and how well you get on with others; your ability and knowledge to do the job.

It is believed that 60% of success is based on attitude and 40% on your skills and knowledge. Your skills and knowledge will take you into the boardroom and into the presence of great people. However, it is your attitude that will keep you there.

Many people have an excellent attitude towards others but their attitude towards themselves is negative. They do not believe in themselves and are constantly negative about themselves. If you have all the skills and knowledge in the world but your attitude is poor, no one will want to work, live or socialise with you. Who would you prefer to work with?

1. Someone with all the skills and knowledge but who disrespects you, your staff and customers?
2. Someone without the skills and knowledge but who has the right attitude and willingness to learn?

Here are the 3 E's that give the perfect mix for managing, developing and accelerating your ASK:

Education    10%    on courses and reading

Exposure    20%    on different roles and getting feedback

Experience  70%    on-the-job experiences, tasks and
                   problem solving

Top executives spend approximately 10% of their time and earnings on educating and investing in themselves. They attend courses, read books, watch videos, listen to audios and take advice from others. They realise that in the multitude of counsellors there is great safety.

The more you expose yourself to different occupations, cultures, countries, food or people, the more you expand your mind. The more you expose yourself to different roles and receive feedback, the more you learn. Learn to love feedback.

One of the best forms of training in the workplace is on-the-job training. In today's marketplace experience plays a significant role. That is why head-hunting is commonplace, because companies are looking for people who have the experience.

Take total control of your personal development and invest in yourself wisely, every day. Identify your aims, design a one-year training and development plan, action it and review it regularly. Maximise the 3 E's, develop your 'ASK' and become the best that you can be.

Never forget the four principles to greater success: aim, plan, action and review. It is a cycle that revolves and is used often by top executives. Use it in difficult conversations or to plan your small or large projects. This tip alone is worth £1000's.

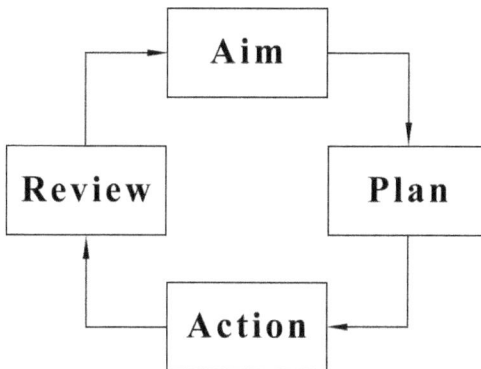

```
        ┌──→  Aim  ──┐
        │            │
        │            ▼
     Review        Plan
        ▲            │
        │            │
        └─ Action ←──┘
```

# Improve
# Your
# Mindset

## Chapter Eleven

*L*earn to master and control your mind, or it will master and control your life and your time. Your mind is one of the most powerful resources that you may ever have in your lifetime. You have no control over anyone else's thinking but your own.

We eventually become like the thoughts we think and the words we speak. What kind of person would you become if you constantly thought negatively about yourself and your situations? Many websites state that the human brain produces between 12,000 and 70,000 thoughts every day, of which 70% are negative. Use this powerful mindset tip to vastly improve your desire to resolve any conflict without delay. Never again say any of the following:

- I have a difficult conversation to deal with
- I have a problem
- I have a challenge

Instead use the following mindset statement, "I have an opportunity." Words convey feelings and feelings lead to action. Therefore be careful what you say or think. See problems and challenges as opportunities.

When we think of a difficult conversation as a problem, it gives the impression of something negative. When we use the word challenge, it suggests hard work. However, when we think of opportunity, we think of benefit. Never again say, "I have a difficult conversation to deal with." Instead say, "I have an opportunity conversation to deal with." The situation remains the same, the only thing that improves is your mindset. What we tell ourselves over a consistently long period of time, we tend to believe and then act out. Look after your mind like a gardener looks after a beautiful garden. Your position in life could be because of the dominating thoughts that have occupied your mind over the years. Garbage in, garbage out.

**Positive Affirmations**

Create a list of positive affirmations and repeat them out loud every morning and evening. I strongly recommend that you list at least ten positive affirmations and repeat them every day to yourself. Affirmations are positive statements that are repeated many times, in order to force the subconscious mind into positive action. These statements must be stated with:

**A**    Attention
**C**    Conviction
**I**    Interest
**D**    Desire

Supposing you are running the marathon for your favourite charity. Seven miles into the race you begin to say to yourself, "I cannot do this." "I am feeling too much pain." "Suppose I get a heart attack?" This type of thinking may cause you to slow down or even stop running.

Positive affirmation will change those thoughts to, "This is easy for me to do." "I love running and I am good at it." "My charity will receive all the funds." "Winners never quit and quitters never win." Some top athletes use positive affirmations from start to finish in their races. They are constantly talking positively to themselves. If you think you are going to have a difficult conversation, the chances are you may.

How is your state of mind? Train your mind to consistently think, "I will", "I can", "I have" and "I am." Let the concept of yourself be continually positive and tell yourself positive things every day. Set positive affirmations for all the following areas of your life:

- Health
- Personal development
- Community
- Career
- Family
- Finance
- Social
- Spiritual

Here are some positive affirmations that top executives and managers use throughout the day:

- I am an effective leader
- I always fulfil my targets, goals and objectives
- I am an effective communicator
- I always have a strategic plan
- I am an effective delegator
- I always evaluate, review and appraise
- I am a team player
- I love to embrace change
- I have integrity
- I am influential

- I am courageous
- I view problems as opportunities and solve them
- I am confident, motivated, enthusiastic and excited
- I am getting better every day
- I love working with all kinds of people
- I am approachable and people admire me
- I am full of wisdom, knowledge and understanding
- I am empathic, caring and assertive
- I work hard and play hard
- I have inner resources, strength and power
- I love working for this company
- I have the right attitude, skills and knowledge

All of these affirmations are stated positively, in the past or present tense because of their greater impact. You can use future tense also.

These affirmations are to be repeated constantly to yourself and not to other people. Their purpose is to drive your subconscious mind into action and not to be arrogant or boastful.

The image you constantly think about yourself will eventually be played out in your life and it may affect everyone around you. Who paints the picture in your mind of yourself for you? Be careful how you see yourself. What you see is what you may experience.

Beware of the environment in which you work and live. Your senses pick up and send information from your environment to your mind, whether negative or positive. As you meditate on the things in your mind it generates how you feel. Your feelings influence your actions and your actions determine the results you achieve. Finally your results will determine your destiny. Your mindset is greatly influenced by your environment.

Here is the pathway to your destiny:


**Environment**

**Senses**

**Mind**

**Feelings**

**Actions**

**Results**

**Destiny**


"You cannot prevent the birds from flying over your head, but you can prevent them from building nests in your hair." *(Chinese Proverb)*

Do not allow anything to be built up in your mind that could eventually destroy you and others. Do everything in your power to change or improve your environment.

# Solve It

## Chapter Twelve

*W*hen you recognise conflict, locate the root cause immediately then destroy it. Do not let it mature and produce ill-will and negativity. More importantly, if you let the day end before you solve it, you may live to regret it.

Conflicts that are left to grow become mountains to destroy. Think how much easier it is to cut down a small plant in comparison to a fully grown tree. Unresolved conflicts that are left for a long time are much more difficult to solve.

What is your conflict management style? Are you the:

- Accommodator?
- Avoider?
- Compromiser?
- Competitor?
- Collaborator?

# Conflict Management Styles

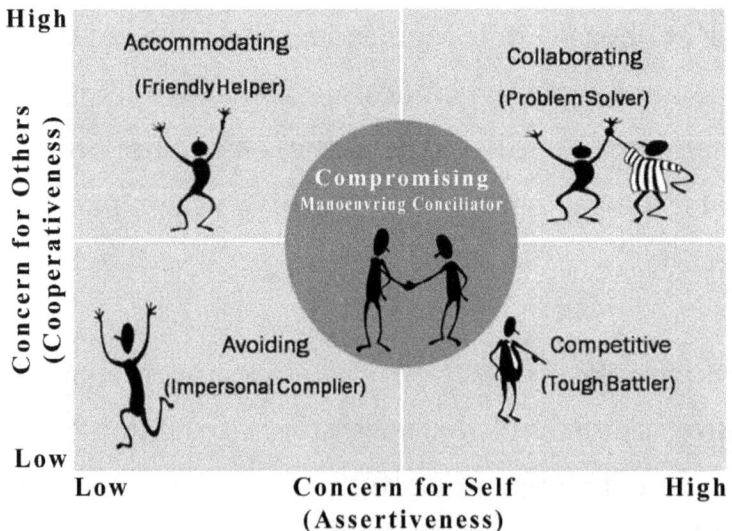

*(Thomas-Kilmann, Conflict Management Styles)*

- The accommodator is unassertive and cooperative
- The avoider is unassertive and uncooperative
- The compromiser is moderate in both assertiveness and cooperativeness
- The competitor is assertive and uncooperative
- The collaborator is both assertive and cooperative

How do you deal with difficult, irrational, aggressive, disrespecting or abusive people, especially those in authority?

**The Know-It-All**

They are arrogant, talkative and very defensive, especially when they are wrong.

**The Passives**

Their common phrase is, I'm not ok, you're ok. They contribute very little and bottle up everything inside.

## The Open And Concealed Aggressor

Their common phrase is, I'm ok, you're not ok. They will walk all over you to get what they want, openly or subtly.

## The Yes People

Quick to say yes and slow to deliver.

## The No People

These are the people who are quick to point out how something cannot work.

## The Dictators

Experts at manipulating, bullying and intimidating others.

## The Gripers

They sit in the seat of the judge but never give praise. They complain, find faults and make others feel uncomfortable.

Ponder these thoughts carefully:

1.   Everyone is difficult sometimes
2.   You may encounter one difficult person every week for the rest of your life
3.   A difficult person can express conflicting behaviour through nonverbal communication
4.   People can show negative or conflicting behaviour without knowing that they are doing so
5.   You may not know when the next difficult person you meet may attack you
6.   Difficult people find it hard to cope with positive people
7.   A difficult person is someone who does not behave the way you want them to

Be a collaborator and solve problems using this amazing tip called FACE RAP. Following this strategy will also give you greater influence over the most difficult kinds of people.

**F**   Fault

**A**   Appearance

**C**   Cause

**E**   Effect


**R**   Responsibility

**A**   Action

**P**   Prevention

## Fault

Every conflict has a root cause or a motive. Detectives often say, "If we can find the motive we can solve the case quicker." When a conflict occurs, your priority should be to locate the motive or root cause immediately and solve it. Locating the root cause or the motive of a conflict can be very challenging.

Become like a detective in a criminal inquiry. Firstly, ask questions, listen and round up all the facts. Secondly, examine the evidence. Thirdly, make a decision and solve the case. Finally, document and follow up.

## Appearance

The appearance of a conflict is in fact the symptom. The symptom indicates that something is wrong. How did the conflict come to your attention? Was it something you saw, heard, felt, smelt or tasted which gave the indication that something was wrong? What was the sign and how did it manifest itself? Maybe it was the look on your colleague's face, the scratch on your car, the pain in your stomach, the flood in your office or your child's school report.

By treating the symptoms you are only providing temporary relief. Investigate and be absolutely certain that something is wrong. The appearance or symptom is the indicator that there is a fault or motive. Without the appearance you will never know that there is a fault.

**Cause**

Conflicts cannot occur without a cause. At this stage your job is to find out who or what was the cause. A group of people or an individual perhaps? Was it the storm, or simply the rain or lightning? Was it the government or your organisation? Identifying who or what caused the conflict puts you in a better position to find the motive or root of the matter.

**Effect**

Every conflict has an effect. Sometimes the effect is minor but on other occasions it can be quite severe. Ask yourself:

- What effect has this conflict had on me, my colleagues, the department or even the whole organisation?
- If I were to leave this conflict unresolved what effect would it have?
- Would today's conflict that remains unresolved be a

cause of tomorrow's conflict?

Today we can see the effects of conflict as it destroys individuals' working relationships. Before the day is out do your very best to resolve the conflict. If it is possible, work in harmony with everyone.

**Responsibility**

At this stage you need to identify who is responsible for taking the appropriate action. The responsibility is dependent upon the type of conflict and may rest with more than one person. Once the person has been identified, the next step is to take action.

**Action**

You have now become like a judge who has listened carefully and patiently to the prosecution and the defence. You have asked questions, weighed up all the relevant facts and taken into consideration the evidence. You have listened to all the witnesses and are now fully informed about the whole situation. You are now in a position to take action but first, brainstorm ways in which you could resolve the conflict. Then evaluate each idea, choosing the best one. Trust your judgement, you will know what is best. From time to time review your actions to see if this was the right choice, if not change it if possible. Finally, ask yourself, "What lessons have been learnt as a result of this conflict?" "What mistakes have I and others made?" Do not allow this learning opportunity to pass you by.

## Prevention

Prevention is better than cure. Ask yourself, how can I prevent this conflict from ever happening again? Look for ways to prevent the conflict from recurring. To continue to repeat the same mistakes is a sign of negligence, incompetence and bad time management. A sign of insanity is, "Doing the same thing over and over again and expecting a different result."

# TIPS Index

**A**  Action it
**R**  Review it
**T**  Teach it

$\mathcal{U}$se the above threefold method (ART) to never forget what you have learnt from this book.

Action the TIPS immediately. Review them every day for 21 days, then twice weekly, twice monthly and then twice a year. Teach and share them with colleagues, family and friends. What you persist in doing becomes easier to do.

There are many TIPS in this book to choose from. Only 50 have been entered into the TIPS index for quick reference.

# Conclusion

*A*ll Scholar International training programmes can be presented on your premises anywhere in the world. They can be exclusively for your personnel and modified in content and objectives to meet your organisation's specific needs.

Our competitive advantages are our ability to entertain our audience, encouraging them to remember what they have learnt. We use tried, tested and proven methods that can be applied immediately. Our passion is to train others to unleash their wealth of potential.

## Scholar International Courses Portfolio

1.  Advanced Neuro Linguistic Programming (NLP)
2.  Advanced Negotiation Skills
3.  Advanced Presentation And Public Speaking Skills
4.  Assertiveness Skills
5.  Business Planning Skills
6.  Customer Care
7.  Creative Thinking And Problem Solving
8.  Communication And The Art Of Listening
9.  Conflict Management
10. Delegation
11. Dealing With Difficult People
12. Dealing With Procrastination
13. Goal Setting
14. Health And Fitness
15. First Line Management
16. Certificate In Management
17. Managing Difficult Conversations
18. Marketing And Selling
19. Meetings For Success
20. One-To-One Coaching And Mentoring

21. Personal Development
22. Professional Telephone Skills
23. Pursuing Excellence Weekend Away
24. Stress And Pressure Management
25. Team Building
26. Team Leadership
27. Train the Trainer
28. Time Management
29. Understanding And Mastering The Internet
30. Writing Skills

To contact the author or enquire about our courses
please write to:

Errol A Williams
Scholar International


Bridge Park
Brentfield Harrow Road
Stonebridge Park
London NW10 0RG
Email: scholar.uk@virgin.net
Website: www.excelling.org

# Notes

Notes

# Notes

Notes

Notes

Notes

www.ingramcontent.com/pod-product-compliance
Lightning Source LLC
Chambersburg PA
CBHW071148200326
41519CB00018B/5159